HISTORIC PHOTOS OF
HEROES OF THE
OLD WEST

TEXT AND CAPTIONS BY MIKE COX

TURNER
PUBLISHING COMPANY

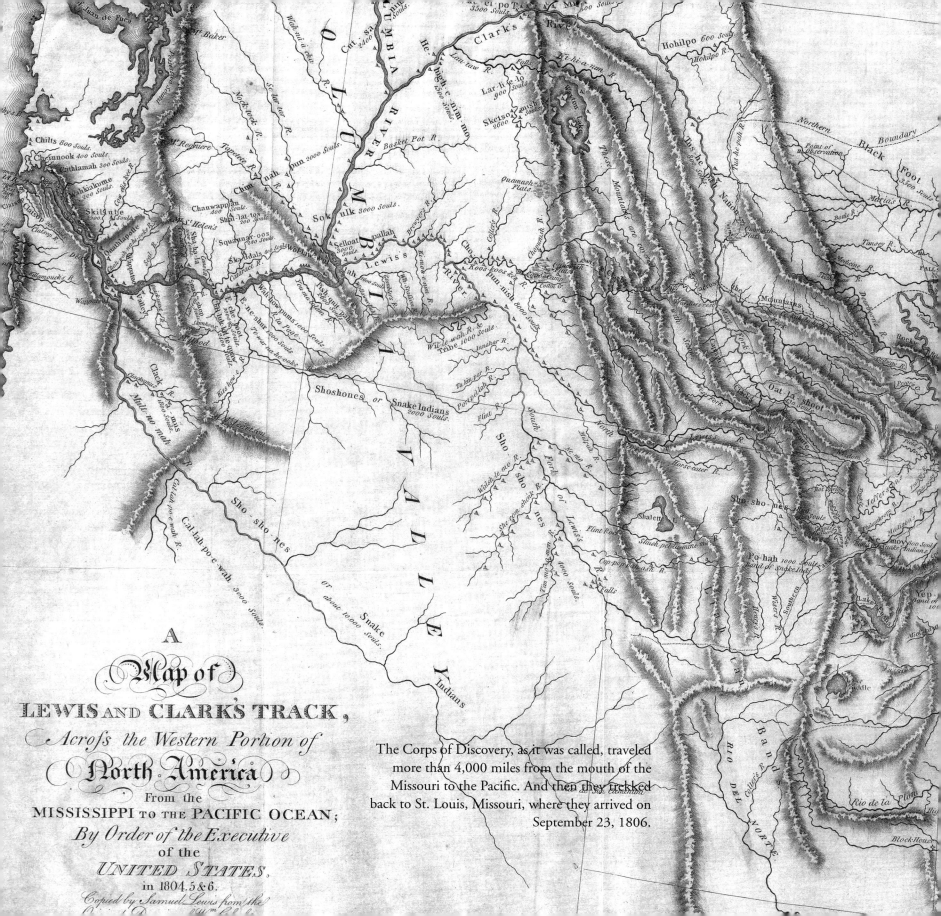

A

Map of

LEWIS AND CLARK'S TRACK,

Across the Western Portion of

North America

From the

MISSISSIPPI TO THE PACIFIC OCEAN;

By Order of the Executive

of the

UNITED STATES,

in 1804.5 & 6.

Copied by Samuel Lewis from the

The Corps of Discovery, as it was called, traveled more than 4,000 miles from the mouth of the Missouri to the Pacific. And then they trekked back to St. Louis, Missouri, where they arrived on September 23, 1806.

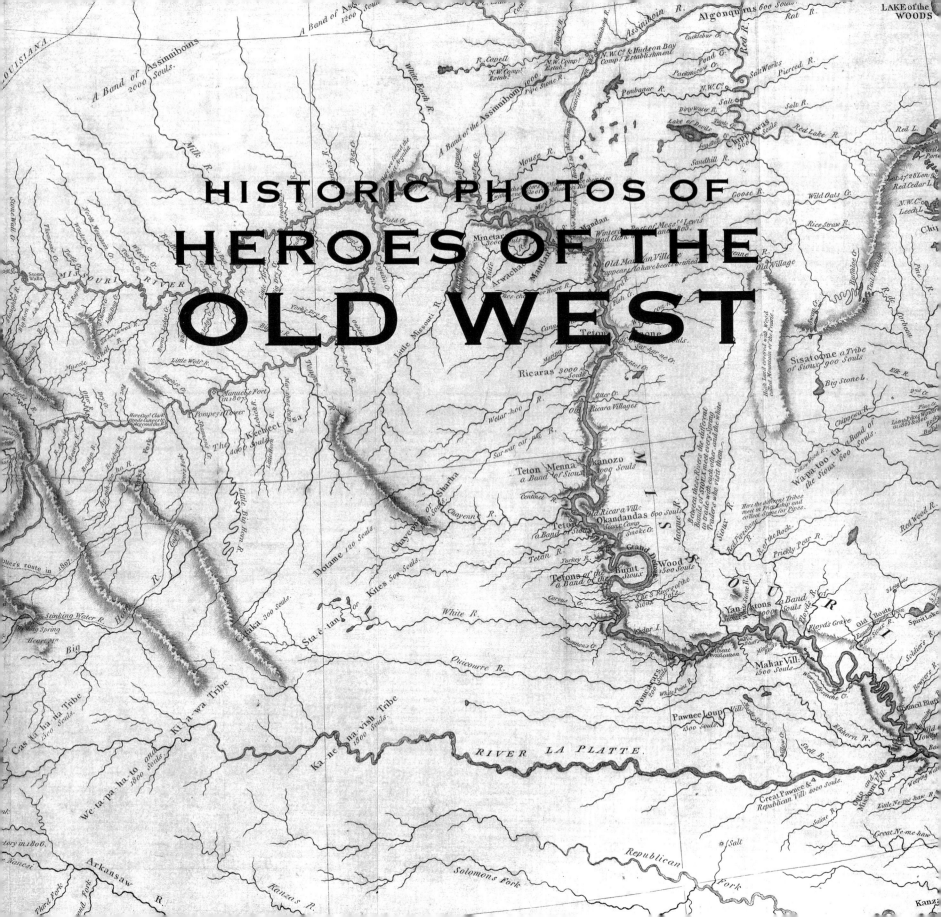

HISTORIC PHOTOS OF
HEROES OF THE
OLD WEST

Turner Publishing Company
200 4th Avenue North • Suite 950
Nashville, Tennessee 37219
(615) 255-2665

www.turnerpublishing.com

Historic Photos of Heroes of the Old West

Library of Congress Control Number: 2009939389

ISBN: 978-1-59652-568-9

Printed in China

10 11 12 13 14 15 16—0 9 8 7 6 5 4 3 2 1

CONTENTS

Stephen Harriman Long (1784–1864), as an officer in the U.S. Army's Topographical Engineers, explored the West during various expeditions from 1817 to 1821. In his most ambitious trek he led an entourage of soldiers, scientists, artists, and topographers on an exploration of the Rockies, the upper Arkansas River, the Red River, and the Canadian River. While he oversaw the gathering of considerable data, Long famously concluded that the West amounted to a great desert unsuited for settlement.

Acknowledgments

This volume, *Historic Photos of Heroes of the Old West,* is the result of the cooperation and efforts of many individuals and organizations. It is with great thanks that we acknowledge the valuable contribution of the following for their generous support:

Denver Public Library
Library of Congress
Mike Cox
National Archives and Records Administration
University of Oklahoma Libraries
University of Texas at San Antonio, Institute of Texan Cultures
Wikimedia Commons

PREFACE

It's easy to look at history simply as a succession of events and dates. But with the exception of natural phenomena like earthquakes, significant occurrences—be they great discoveries or brutal massacres—do not happen without people.

The saga of America's westward movement is the story of people, many of whom we can consider heroes and heroines. Not that the Old West didn't have plenty of rascals, from scalp hunters to outlaws and crooked businessmen and politicians, but the heroes were the ones who explored, settled, spanned, and civilized the West.

Though the story of the American West is as big as the West itself, when it comes to heroes, they can be grouped into five broad categories: The pathfinders who literally blazed the trails for others to follow as a young nation pursued what some considered its Manifest Destiny to span the North American continent from the Atlantic to the Pacific; the pioneers of various stripe who followed; the builders and innovators who spanned the continent with improved means of transportation and communication or provided the tools to tame it; the civilizers who settled things down; and last, the perpetrators of the Western myth, a story that hardly needed embellishment but got it anyway.

The earliest Western exploration occurred before the invention of photography, but the technology existed in time to capture some of the pathfinders as older men. As the state of the photographic art continued to grow along with the West, the time considered to be the peak of the epoch—the last half of the nineteenth century—was well documented by men who captured images on emulsion-covered glass plates.

Human drama needs a stage, both figuratively and literally. With the story of the Old West, the action unfolds on a stage that extends westward from the Mississippi River to the Pacific Ocean, an area that now includes 23 states not counting Hawaii. But the eastern tier of Western states—Minnesota, Iowa, Missouri, Arkansas, and Louisiana—didn't stay western for long. In the collective imagination of most Americans, the real West begins on a line from North Dakota to Texas where relatively flat land reaches for the Rocky Mountains and beyond.

The acquisition of most of this vast territory boils down to four big land deals, starting with the Louisiana Purchase in 1803. That year, in consideration of $11.25 million in actual cost and another $8 million in assumed debt, President Thomas Jefferson signed off on the purchase of some eight million square miles from France. For roughly four cents an acre, the U.S. had doubled in size.

In 1845, the United States annexed the independent Republic of Texas, making it the 28th state. Following the war with Mexico that development brought about, in negotiations completed in 1850, the U.S. acquired all or part of the land that eventually became the states of California, Nevada, Arizona, Utah, Colorado, and New Mexico. In between, the nation got title to the Oregon Territory from Great Britain in 1846. That included the future states of Washington, Oregon, and Idaho.

Not quite 50 years later, in 1893, historian Frederick Jackson Turner gave a speech in Chicago in which he declared the frontier dead. But the Indian Territory (Oklahoma), New Mexico, and Arizona did not lose their territorial status and become states until the first and second decades of the twentieth century. Some say the Old West lived on in some places until the United States entered the First World War in 1917.

Visitors can still find plenty of wide open space in the West, some of it still rugged and remote, but in the twenty-first century, the Old West lives only in our collective imagination—and in old photographs.

—Mike Cox

Virginia-born Joseph Lafayette Meek (1810–1875) explored the Rocky Mountains as a fur trapper with William Sublette of the Rocky Mountain Fur Company, surviving brushes with hostile Indians and an attack by a grizzly bear.

THE PATHFINDERS

When France conveyed its vast North American territory to the United States in spring 1803, Napoleon Bonaparte had no real idea what he had just sold, and President Jefferson had little knowledge of the huge chunk of the continent just acquired. Some Americans even believed that prehistoric woolly mammoths still trod the slopes of the far West's mountains. To learn as much as possible about the new land, Jefferson commissioned Meriwether Lewis, an Army captain, to head an expedition to study the new possession firsthand. Lewis chose William Clark to accompany him. With 38 men including an Indian guide, as well as a small group of Frenchmen to serve as couriers to return letters and botanical specimens, the Corps of Discovery left Illinois on May 14, 1804, for a voyage up the Missouri River and on into the Pacific Northwest. The Lewis and Clark expedition, which reached the ocean on November 7, 1805, and made it back to civilization on September 23, 1806, was the first of numerous explorations over the next half-century.

Zebulon Pike departed on an extensive Western reconnaissance on July 15, 1806. He discovered and named Pike's Peak in Colorado. Mainly due to the War of 1812, Western exploration stalled until 1820, when Army major Stephen H. Long made another survey of the Arkansas and Red river basins. Long and his men gathered useful information, but the major made one blunder: He labeled the Great Plains the "Great American Desert" and declared it uninhabitable. The next wave of exploration would be driven by capitalism. Hats made of beaver skin had become all the rage back east and the virgin streams in the West teemed with the suddenly valuable buck-toothed animals. Beginning with John Colter, a former member of the Lewis and Clark party, men content to make a dangerous living trapping beaver penetrated the Rocky Mountains and the river basins of the West. These Mountain Men were soon followed by bold traders like Charles and William Bent, who set up remote trading posts that stimulated more commerce. John C. Fremont led expeditions to survey the Oregon Territory and California. With the soon-to-be legendary Kit Carson as his guide, Fremont gathered information that set off widespread immigration to the Pacific Northwest. John Wesley Powell, a one-armed Civil War veteran, led the last great Western exploration in 1869 when he headed the first known float trip down the Colorado through what would become known as the Grand Canyon. The pathfinders had blazed trails that became well worn as Americans spread across the continent like a wind-blown prairie fire.

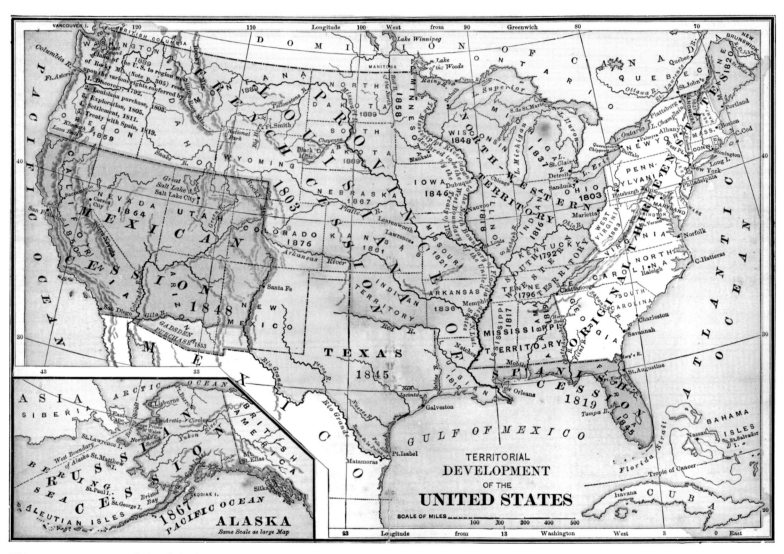

This 1890 map, prepared shortly before historian Frederick Jackson famously declared the American frontier dead, shows how the United States tripled in area from 1803 to 1848.

Meriwether Lewis (left), born in Virginia in 1774, led the so-called Lewis and Clark expedition to explore the huge expanse of new western land acquired by the United States in the 1803 Louisiana Purchase. William Clark, right, was Lewis' co-commander.

The Lewis and Clark expedition encountered numerous Indians on their journey to the Pacific Northwest. On August 3, 1804, they met with a delegation of Missouri and Otoe Indians near present Omaha, Nebraska, the first official interaction between the United States and any western tribe.

As this imagined engraving shows, John Colter famously saved his scalp by running barefoot—and bareskinned—from Indians. He escaped death that time, but he died young of natural causes in 1813. Colter was first to describe the geysers and other geothermal activity of the Yellowstone region of Wyoming and is widely dubbed the first mountain man.

Zebulon Pike and his men wintered in Colorado, and then moved south. A hundred Spanish dragoons approached the explorers on February 26, 1807, and asked Pike what he was doing. The captain said he was exploring the Red River, but in actuality, he was on the Rio Grande. Believing at first that he was a spy, Spanish authorities confiscated Pike's maps and other materials and held him until July 1. He later published an account of his expedition, relying only on memory.

General Pike.

A New Yorker, Jedediah Strong Smith (1799–1831) came west in 1822 as a fur trader employed by Missouri lieutenant governor General William Henry Ashley. He relocated the South Pass through the Rockies and was reputedly the first white man to travel in the regions of Nevada and Utah, the first American in California, and an early explorer of Oregon. Smith survived a vicious encounter with a grizzly bear, but in May 1831 Comanches killed him on the Santa Fe Trail.

When mountain man Jim Bridger (1804–1881) found a huge body of salty water, he thought he had discovered the Pacific Ocean. Actually, he had discovered the Great Salt Lake. Using charcoal on dried, stretched buffalo hide, Bridger made some of the early West's most accurate maps. He spent two decades as a fur trapper and later became a trader.

Born in Virginia in 1810, Joseph Lafayette Meek took up farming in Oregon, playing an important role in lobbying Congress for Oregon statehood. He served as a sheriff and later was elected to the territorial legislature. In 1848, Meek gained appointment as the territory's U.S. marshal, a job he kept for five years. This is how he looked in 1853.

James P. Beckwourth (ca. 1800–1866) was the son of a revolutionary war veteran and a mulatto slave. His family moved to the St. Louis area in 1810, where two years later he was apprenticed to a blacksmith. When Beckwourth was in his twenties, his father sought and received deeds of emancipation on his behalf, transforming him into a freeman. This is the only known photograph of Beckwourth, who became a hunter and trapper, taken in Denver around 1860. Six years later he left on a hunting expedition with Crows and died, possibly of food poisoning. With the advent of the civil rights movement more than a century later, Beckwourth was finally acknowledged as one of the West's earliest African-American pioneers.

Beckwourth went to work for the Rocky Mountain Fur Company in 1824. Four years later, at a mountain man rendezvous, he married into the Crow Indian tribe, living in what is now Montana while trapping beaver for the fur company. Having moved farther west, in 1851 he discovered a route through the Sierra Nevada Mountains later named Beckwourth Pass in his honor. In this engraving, which appeared in his 1856 memoir, Beckwourth tangles with a bear.

Eng.d by J. C. Buttre. N.Y.

In 1841, Congress approved $30,000 in funding for a military expedition to map a route to Oregon. Thanks to the fact that the powerful senator from Missouri, Thomas Hart Benton, was his father-in-law, 29-year-old John Charles Freemont (1813–1890), got the assignment to lead the foray. Beginning in the spring of 1842, the trek resulted in a series of seven highly serviceable maps and made army topographical engineer Freemont famous.

By the time Freemont posed for this studio portrait in the late 1850s or early 1860s, he had led a total of five explorations of the West. Though called the Great Pathfinder, he wasn't infallible. In an effort to find a future railroad route through the Rockies, in 1848 he got caught in a winter storm and lost 11 of his men. Fremont would run unsuccessfully for President in 1856.

When Fremont mapped the Oregon Trail, Kit Carson (1809–1868) rode ahead as his guide. Born in Kentucky, Carson grew up in Missouri. He came west in 1826, working variously as a wagoneer, trapper, hunter, and scout. Carson was later depicted in this fanciful dime novel cover illustration.

Carson's service with Fremont's 1842 expedition made him famous, but that fame continued to grow. He carried news of the California gold discovery to Washington in 1849, fought Indians, and served as a colonel of New Mexico volunteers during the Civil War. By then, he had settled near Taos, where he spent most of the rest of his life.

This is how Santa Fe, New Mexico, looked during Kit Carson's time. The image shows the east side of the plaza in 1866.

John Wesley Powell (1834–1902), who lost most of one arm to a Civil War wound, led the 1869 geographic expedition of the Green and Colorado rivers. The three-month river trip included a float down the Colorado through the Grand Canyon, a massive geologic feature previously known only to Indians.

Powell's first camp, a spot in the willows along the Green River in Wyoming Territory.

When Powell conducted his exploration, his primary objective was to map the topography and do a geological survey, but he also documented the native cultures he encountered. In this image, a group of Paiute men and boys are sitting in a large circle around two white men, one of them Major Powell. The photograph was taken on the Kaibab Plateau near the Grand Canyon in northern Arizona.

John K. Hillers works with negatives in camp, Utah Territory, as a member of John Wesley Powell's second geological survey, which departed in 1871 in a bid to map the territory explored by Powell on his first expedition in 1869. Joining the group as a boatman, Hillers became Powell's chief expedition photographer and is credited with some of the earliest photographs of the Grand Canyon.

In this fanciful engraving, a buckskin-clad hunter is joining two Indians on a buffalo hunt. By 1880, the bison, which once roamed the West in the hundreds of thousands, had nearly become extinct.

Professional buffalo hunters roamed the Great Plains, killing the great beasts for their hides while often leaving the rest of the animal to waste. Buffalo being a large component of the Plains Indian diet, the slaughter made life much harder on the various tribes and stimulated bloody reprisals.

Large Sioux Indian camp on Brule River near the Pine Ridge, South Dakota. This image was recorded in January 1891, preserving for posterity what a Plains Indian village looked like.

A member of the Wheeler Expedition, which set off in 1871 to explore the territories of Idaho, Colorado, New Mexico, and Arizona, sketches Anasazi ruins at Canyon de Chelly. Timothy O'Sullivan, a government photographer well known for his images of Civil War battlefields, was along for the journey and captured this image in 1872.

Following in the footsteps of Zebulon Pike, these climbers are rounding Windy Point on their way to the summit of Pike's Peak in Colorado around 1890. Pike himself never reached the summit, but his account of his expedition into the Southwest, published in 1810, was relied on by all nineteenth-century explorers heading west.

COLT'S NEW MODEL ARMY METALLIC CARTRIDGE REVOLVING PISTOL.

Catalog engraving of the weapon that arguably won the West, the six-shot revolver invented and manufactured by Samuel Colt.
This model, manufactured for the Army but wildly popular with civilians, cost $20.

THE PIONEERS

Though fur trappers and traders had been operating in the Rocky Mountains and Pacific Northwest since 1807, the first wave of permanent settlers did not come to the West until 1821. That year, young Stephen F. Austin fulfilled his late father Moses' dream and brought 300 American colonists to settle between the Brazos and Colorado rivers in Texas. A longtime possession of Spain, Texas had recently become a province of the new republic of Mexico. By 1834, roughly 30,000 settlers had come to the region from the United States, compared with only 8,000 or so from Mexico. On March 2, 1836, Texas declared its independence from Mexico but it took Sam Houston's defeat of General Antonio Lopez de Santa Anna at San Jacinto on April 21 to make that declaration a reality.

Halfway across the continent from Texas, the land encompassing the future states of Oregon, Washington, and Idaho began to settle up in the 1830s and early 1840s. By 1843, immigrants streamed westward along the Oregon Trail. In the spring of 1847 Brigham Young led a vanguard of 148 fellow Mormons to the valley formed by the Great Salt Lake in what would become Utah. In a land Young and his followers called Deseret, an area which included Utah and parts of Arizona, California, Nebraska, and Nevada, almost a hundred Mormon settlements eventually arose. The largest was Salt Lake City, a community Young proclaimed Zion, "the seat of God's kingdom on earth." Young had gone west seeking a religious kingdom, but a golden idol soon attracted many thousands more.

The first American settlers had begun arriving in California, still part of Mexico, in 1841. But the accidental discovery of gold on the American River above John Sutter's trading post at what is now Sacramento triggered one of the largest mass migrations in history, the California gold rush of 1849–1850.

The last big wave of settlement, the Oklahoma Land Rush, came in 1889 when President Benjamin Harrison opened to white settlement the unoccupied land in the Indian Territory. A gunshot at noon on April 22 that year signaled hopeful settlers that they could cross the border and stake their claims. Inside nine hours, some two million acres of tribal land had been claimed as individual tracts, though much of the better land had already been taken by folks who slipped in early, a group of settlers who came to be called "Sooners."

Known as the Father of Texas, Stephen F. Austin (1793–1836) brought 300 colonists to the Mexican province of Texas in 1821, the year Mexico fought its way to independence from Spain and began permitting immigration from the U.S. to encourage settlement of the region. That influx of settlers from the United States marked the first significant American toehold in the West.

The chapel of the old Spanish mission of San Antonio de Valero, better known as the Alamo, became a world icon for heroism in defense of freedom following the fall of the historic fortress on March 6, 1836. Some 185 men died at the hands of a much larger force of Mexican troops while fighting for Texas independence.

Virginia-born Sam Houston (1794–1863) came to Texas in 1833 from Tennessee. Three years later, on April 21, 1836, he ensured Texas' independence from Mexico by defeating the army of General Antonio Lopez de Santa Anna at San Jacinto. Houston was soon elected the first president of the new Republic of Texas.

One of the Old West's most enduring stories began in 1836 with the capture of young Cynthia Ann Parker after Comanches attacked her family's log fort in what is now Limestone County, Texas. She lived with the Indians until 1860 when she was recaptured by Texas Rangers. In this often retouched image, she is shown nursing her daughter Toh-Tsee-Ah after her unenthusiastic return to white society. She died, never having adjusted to her new life, around 1870.

Following John C. Fremont's expedition in 1842, Americans began moving west en masse on the Oregon Trail, a route that stretched 2,000 miles from Missouri through Kansas, Nebraska, Wyoming, and Idaho. The trail went along the Platte River to its headwaters and then crossed the Rocky Mountains. In Idaho, the trail split with one branch going to California and the other along the Snake River to the Columbia, which empties into the Pacific.

Brigham Young (1801–1877) joined the Church of Jesus Christ of Latter-day Saints in New York in 1832. When church founder Joseph Smith was murdered in 1844 in Nauvoo, Illinois, Young took over as leader of the Mormons. Three years later, Young led 148 followers westward to the Great Salt Lake in Utah.

Though the first wave of Mormons to occupy the West were not photographed on their way, a photographer named C. W. Carter later captured this image of a wagon train of Mormon settlers. Thousands of Mormons traveled the old Oregon Trail to Salt Lake, which soon became Salt Lake City.

Volunteers quarry granite in 1872 at Cottonwood Canyon for the Mormon Temple being built in Salt Lake City. Construction began in 1853 and continued for 40 years. The temple was dedicated in 1893.

In the foreground of this early image of the completed Mormon Temple is the Brigham Young Monument featuring Brigham Young. The monument honors 6,000 pioneers who died on their way west to Utah between 1847 and 1869.

Ann Eliza Webb Young (1844–?) married the Mormon leader when she was 24 and he was 67. She sued him for divorce in 1874 and went on to write a book called *Wife No. 19* which criticized polygamy for its harmful effects on women (Brigham Young reportedly had 55 wives). Ann disappears from history after 1908, but she was an early advocate for women.

Nothing fancy, but this pioneer's log cabin kept the wild animals out and the heat in on a cold winter night.

Dwarfed by John Sutter's log sawmill on the American River in Northern California, James Wilson Marshall (1810–1885) is the man who discovered gold above Sacramento in 1849. Marshall's find triggered the great California gold rush that lured a wave of precious metal–hungry "49ers" westward. Marshall, who never profited from his find, died penniless. This image is from a daguerreotype made around 1850.

Gold was discovered in French Creek near present Custer, South Dakota, in 1874. Within two years, the boom town of Deadwood had sprouted through the tall timber. Stores and shops coexisted with bars and brothels as Deadwood grew to a town of 5,000 almost overnight.

The quest for gold was an important factor in the settlement of the West. Beyond the original California frenzy, gold or silver booms fueled immigration to Colorado, Nevada, the Dakotas, Alaska, and other future states. Prospectors often used burros to haul their gear into remote areas.

Workers near Hillsboro in New Mexico Territory bag ore under a canvas awning outside a mountainside mine shaft. Once bagged, the ore was hand-carried to a wagon drawn by four mules. Gold was discovered in that part of New Mexico in 1877.

The road to instant wealth was long and hard for most of the men who tried their luck, and those who sought gold by mining for it sometimes lived short lives. Sinking a shaft consisted of hammering a spike into the rocks and filling the hole full of dynamite, then repeating the procedure again and again, hoping to strike the mother lode. This miner is chewing into the great Comstock Lode, somewhere below Virginia City, Nevada, around 1867.

In August 1896, rich placer deposits of gold were discovered along Bonanza Creek in the Yukon. As word got out, adventurers lost no time making the trek to the remote wildernesses of Alaska and northwest Canada. The prospectors seen here are packing along the Dyea Trail around 1897.

The quest for precious metal was one factor stimulating western settlement, but the cattle industry played a far more indelible role in opening the West. One of the pioneers of the agri-business model was Charles Goodnight (1836–1929). A former scout and Texas Ranger, he and Oliver Loving blazed the first big cattle trail out of Texas. Goodnight later ranched in the Texas Panhandle and is credited with inventing the chuck wagon. He also led the way in herd improvement through cross-breeding and helped to preserve the buffalo.

A pioneer family pose in front of their covered wagon at Loup Valley, Nebraska, participants in the Great Western migration.

Interior of a schooner wagon at Yolo County, California. The covered wagon was driven out of Cincinnati by John Bemmerly in 1849.

Harper's Weekly magazine billed itself as the "Journal of Civilization," but it often provided coverage on the portion of the continent that was the last to get civilized: the West. This cover from 1885 depicts a Mexican *vaquero,* or cowboy.

HARPER'S WEEKLY.
JOURNAL OF CIVILIZATION.

Vol. XXIX.—No. 1487.
Copyright, 1885, by Harper & Brothers.

NEW YORK, SATURDAY, JUNE 20, 1885.

TEN CENTS A COPY.
$4.00 PER YEAR, IN ADVANCE.

"THE LONG DETACHING RINGS AGAIN WRITHED IN MID-AIR, AND SOFTLY DESCENDED AS HE THUNDERED PAST."—[SEE SERIAL "MARUJA," PAGE 396.]

Two typical cowboys, one of them ready to throw a loop, were photographed by a professional photographer in New Mexico in the mid-1880s.

Not every cowboy tended cattle while armed, but this waddy posing astride his horse somewhere in the Dakota Territory in the late 1870s or early 1880s carried a lever-action rifle in his saddle scabbard and a revolver on his hip.

Where and when this image was captured is not recorded, but somewhere along the way someone titled it, "Cowboy looking for a job." He's leading a spare horse packing his bedding.

This image of a cattle roundup was recorded in Kansas, but it could have been almost anywhere in the West when the cowboy was becoming an American icon.

Being a cowboy involved more than wearing a big hat and pointy-toed boots. One job skill, demonstrated by this long-haired puncher in the mid-1890s on a ranch in Graham County, Arizona Territory, involved throwing a loop to lasso a steer.

The life story of John Slaughter (1841–1922) encapsulates the history of the Southwest. Though born in Louisiana, he came to Texas as a youth with his family when it was still an independent republic. As a young man, he worked as a cowboy and rode as a Texas Ranger before moving to Arizona Territory in 1878. Six years later, he bought the 65,000-acre San Bernardino land grant, which he ranched for the rest of his long life. He also served as sheriff of Cochise County for a time.

Nat Love (1854–1921) was a pioneer cowboy. Born into slavery, after selling a horse he won in a lottery, he left his native Tennessee and went to Dodge City, Kansas, to be a cowboy. Love went on to work on ranches in Texas, South Dakota, and Arizona before settling down in the Lone Star state, where he spent the rest of his life. In 1907, he wrote an autobiography, *Life and Adventures of Nat Love.*

Born in Texas to a black father and Mexican mother, Benjamin Hodges (1856–1929) arrived in Dodge City, Kansas, on a cattle drive in 1872. He may have made a tolerable trail hand, but his real talent lay in being a cattle thief, card cheat, and confidence man. One thing that can be said for him, he survived for a long time in a town not known for the longevity of its rougher characters. After his burial in Dodge City's Maple Grove Cemetery, one pallbearer said, "We buried Ben there for a good reason. We wanted him where they could keep an eye on him."

This not-too-happy-looking pioneer couple pose for a glass negative studio shot in New Mexico in the mid-1880s. It was the custom of the day for men to take a seat while their wives stood beside them. Including a pet in the image was a bit unusual.

Merchandizing wasn't as glitzy in the Old West as it would become in the next centuries. And for those who've ever visited a "confectionery," spelling could be downright frustrating. This glass plate image was taken in Hillsboro, New Mexico Territory, in the mid-1880s.

An honest dealer could be a hero in the Old West. This is a game of faro at the Orient Saloon in the mining boom town of Bisbee, Arizona. In the nineteenth century, faro outranked poker as the most popular form of gambling.

As settlers spread across the West, some all-wood towns really did look like later-day Hollywood Western sets. This image, originally labeled "Saloons and disreputable places of Hazen [Nevada]" was recorded in 1905. That year postdates the classic days of the Old West, but the West was still pretty wild in places, including towns like this one.

In the arid Southwest, where lumber was scarce and therefore expensive, many settlers followed the old Spanish technique of mixing straw and mud to form sun-dried adobe bricks for their homes and businesses. Though some wood was used, much of Hillsboro, New Mexico Territory, consisted of adobe structures.

The West may have been sparsely settled in the 1880s, but thanks to improved communication and the railroads, women could still keep up with the latest in fashion trends. This flower-topped hat was known as a "three-story" or "flower pot" hat, for obvious reasons. The photograph was made in a New Mexico studio in the mid-1880s.

Hollywood wardrobe departments seldom get the look of real Old West cowboy hats right. Contrary to Hollywood portrayals over the years, nineteenth-century cowboy hats usually had flat brims with crowns uncreased. This image was recorded in a photography studio in Hillsboro, New Mexico, in the mid-1880s.

Not every man who came to the West looked like a cowboy. This fellow, posing in the mid-1880s, is obviously wearing his Sunday best. He's also wearing that "darned what was it my wife told me to do" expression. Some photographers can trip a shutter at just the right moment.

Following Spread: Much of what is now Oklahoma had been designated as Indian land and was called Indian Territory. But in 1889, the federal government began opening unoccupied land to white settlement on a first-come, first-to-own basis. Troop C, Fifth Cavalry, arrested squatters and those who tried to stake claims before it was legal.

Oklahoma land runs took place in 1889, 1891, 1892, and 1893. One of the boom towns that resulted was Perry, shown here in 1893. In all, the government made 10 million acres of Oklahoma land available for settlement. Those who tried to slip in on new land early came to be called Sooners.

Parceling out millions of acres of former Indian land took a lot of paperwork. The unarmed men in this image are federal clerks working in the U.S. Land Office at Perry. The men with the weapons are deputy U.S. marshals. This image was recorded October 12, 1893.

Guthrie became capital of the newly designated Oklahoma Territory (formerly Indian Territory) in 1889 and rapidly grew to a city of 10,000. It retained its status after Oklahoma became a state in 1907, but three years later Oklahoma City became the seat of state government and Guthrie went into an economic decline that lasted for decades. This image shows Harrison Avenue in May 1893.

THEY SPANNED A CONTINENT

With the addition of the Oregon Territory in 1846, followed two years later by war-weary Mexico's cession of territory to the U.S., the nation finally stretched from ocean to ocean. But that much land could not be controlled without improved transportation and communication. The California gold discovery, which increased settlement and fanned economic activity to the melting point, also created the need for better cross-continent communication. A fast-growing nation found it unacceptable that a first-class letter mailed from San Francisco required a month by ship to reach Washington, D.C.

The first effort at regularly scheduled ground transportation was John Butterfield's Overland Mail Company, which began running stagecoaches between Tipton, Missouri, and San Diego in 1858. The roughly 2,700-mile journey usually took about three weeks. Since a horse could make better progress than a team pulling a wagon, the next effort at ground communication was the Pony Express. Founder William Russell set up more than 150 stations some 15 miles apart and hired slim young men to ride as fast they could between stations, changing to a new horse at each station. On October 24, 1861, eighteen months after Pony Express riders started crisscrossing the West, the nation's first transcontinental telegraph line began carrying messages. Transmitted from Sacramento to Washington, the first telegram to span the continent bore a message to President Abraham Lincoln. The telegraph put the Pony Express out of business, with longer messages once again traveling either by stagecoach or oceangoing vessel. But a faster mode of land transportation was on the horizon.

Despite its preoccupation with the Civil War, the U.S. Congress passed an act in 1862 followed by a broader measure in 1864 providing incentives of land and bonds for a railroad connecting California and the existing railhead at Omaha, Nebraska. By the time President Lincoln signed the second act into law, the Union Pacific had begun laying tracks westward from Omaha to link with the Central Pacific line, which started eastward from Sacramento. The two lines met at Promontory Point, Utah, on May 10, 1869.

As improved transportation and communication knit the nation together, entrepreneurial innovators developed new tools—from blue jeans and Stetson hats to repeating weapons and barbed wire—to help those who hoped to tame the new land. Others came up with inventive new ways to make money.

THE OVERLAND STAGE LINE,

FOR CARRYING THE

GREAT

Through Mails

Ben Holladay.

FROM THE

ATLANTIC

TO THE

Pacific States

Proprietor.

Denver City Dec 6th 1864

Received from *Mess Clark & Co*

in apparent good order, *One Letter with two Packages.* said to contain

Gold Dust valued at Twenty five Thousand ($25000.00) Gold or Sixty two thousand ($62,000.00) Dollars in Treasury notes.

MARKED "

Northrup & Chick. Nassau Street New York city.

IT IS AGREED, and is a part of the consideration of this contract, that the OVERLAND STAGE LINE are not to be held responsible for any loss or damage except as forwarders only ; nor for any loss or damage by the dangers of railroad, ocean or river navigation, leakage, breakage, fire, or from any cause whatever, unless the same be proved to have occurred from the fraud or gross neglect of ourselves, our agents or servants, or unless insured by us, (in no case do we insure against leakage or breakage,) and in no event is this Company to be liable beyond their route as herein receipted. VALUED UNDER FIFTY DOLLARS, unless otherwise herein stated.

ALL KINDS OF FRAGILE WARE AT SHIPPER'S RISK.

For the Overland Stage Line,

Charges 930, 00

C L Dahler

AGENT.

Slote & Janes, Stationers, 93 Fulton Street, N. Y.

Veteran New York stagecoach operator John Butterfield won a $600,000-a-year federal contract in 1857 to carry mail from Missouri to California. Butterfield bought stagecoaches, built way stations across the Southwest, and succeeded in living up to the terms of his contract, which called for getting mail and passengers from St. Louis to the West Coast inside three weeks.

SPECIAL INSTRUCTIONS.

In order to carry out this undertaking, it is necessary that the following Instructions be strictly observed by all Employés of the Company.

TO CONDUCTORS, AGENTS, DRIVERS & EMPLOYÉS.

1.—It is expected that all employés of the Company will be at their posts at all times, in order to guard and protect the property of the Company. Have teams harnessed in ample time, and ready to proceed without delay or confusion. Where the coaches are changed, have the teams hitched to them in time. Teams should be hitched together and led to or from the stable to the coach, so that no delay can occur by their running away. All employés will assist the Driver in watering and changing teams in all cases, to save time.

2.—When a stage is seriously detained by accident or otherwise, the Conductor or Driver will have the same noted on way bill and note book, and report fully to the Superintendent at first station the nature and cause of such delay.

3.—Conductors should never lose sight of the mails for a moment, or leave them, except in charge of the driver or some other employé of the Company, who will guard them till his return. This rule must not be deviated from under *any circumstances*. They will also report to the Superintendent in all cases if Drivers abuse or mis-manage their teams, or in any way neglect or refuse to do their duty.

4.—The time of all employés is expected to be at the disposal of the Company's Agents, in all cases, at stations where they may be laying over. Their time belongs exclusively to the Company; they will therefore be always ready for duty.

5.—None but the Company's Superintendents or Agents who have written permission, are authorized to make or contract debts, give notes, due bills, or any obligations on account of the Company.

6.—Conductors and Drivers will be very particular, and not allow the Company's property to be abused, or neglect to report to the proper parties the repairs required.

7.—You will be particular to see that the mails are protected from the wet, and kept safe from injury of every kind while in your possession, in your division, and you will be held personally responsible for the safe delivery at the end of your route, or point of destination, of all mails and other property in your charge.

8.—The Company will not at present transport any *through* extra baggage, freights, or parcels of any description. All employés are cautioned against receiving such matter in any shape or manner, except such local business of this nature, from place to place, as will be done according to the instructions and prices to be given by the different Superintendents. You will not fail to see that all parcels, boxes or bundles carried on the stage, shall be entered on the way bill, with amount of freight to be charged, and you will be held responsible for the safe delivery, at point of destination, of all such packages. The Agent will see that the charges are paid, and articles receipted for at time of delivery. No money, jewelry, bank notes, or valuables of any nature, will be allowed to be carried under any circumstances whatever.

9.—All Superintendents, Agents, Conductors and Drivers will see particularly that every passenger shall have their names entered on the way-bill at point of departure; that their fare shall be paid in advance, and the amount entered on way-bill as paid to point of destination. No Conductor or Agent must allow any stage to leave his station without personally comparing the way-bill with the passengers, and knowing that they agree. Each Station Agent will be required to note the time of arrival and departure of each stage at his station, both on the way-bill and on a book kept for that purpose, giving the Driver and Conductor's name and cause of delay, if any has occurred.

10.—Superintendents will report to the President and Treasurer of the Company, and to each other, the names of the persons authorised to receipt fare on way-bill. No others than those named by them will be allowed to receipt fare.

11.—The rates of fare will, for the present, be as follows: between the Pacific Railroad terminus and San Francisco, and between Memphis and San Francisco, either way, through tickets, $200. Local fares between Fort Smith and Fort Yuma not less than 10 cents per mile for the distance traveled. Between Fort Yuma and San Francisco, and between Fort Smith and the Railroad terminus, the rate of fare will be published by the Superintendents of those divisions.

12.—The meals and provisions for passengers are at their own expense, over and above the regular fare. The Company intend, as soon as possible, to have suitable meals at proper places prepared for passengers at a moderate cost.

13.—Each passenger will be allowed baggage not exceeding 40 lbs. in any case.

14.—Passengers stopping from one stage to another, can only do so at their own risk as to the Company being able to carry them on a following stage. In cases of this nature, the Conductor or Agent at the place where they leave the stage, will endorse on the way-bill opposite their name, " Stopped over at ———." And on the way-bill of the stage in which the passenger continues his journey, the entry of his name will be made with the remark, " Stopped over from stage of the ——— (giving the date). Fare paid to ——— on way-bill of ——— (date) from——— (name the place.)"

15.—All employés are expected to show proper respect to and treat passengers and the public with civility, as well as to use every exertion for the comfort and convenience of passengers.

16.—Agents, Conductors, Drivers and all employés will follow strictly all instructions that may be received from time to time from the Superintendents of their respective divisions.

17.—Any transactions of a disreputable nature will be sufficient cause for the discharge of any person from the employ of the Company.

18.—INDIANS. A good look-out should be kept for Indians No intercourse should be had with them, but let them alone; by no means annoy or wrong them. At all times an efficient guard should be kept, and such guard should always be *ready* for any emergency.

19.—It is expected of every employé that he will further the interests of the Company by every means in his power, more especially by living on good terms with all his fellow-employés, by avoiding quarrels and disagreements of every kind and nature with all parties, and by the strictest attention of each and every one to his duties.

M. L. KENYON, *San Francisco, Cal.*
HUGH CROCKER, *Fort Smith, Ark.*
JAMES GLOVER, *El Paso, Texas*   } *Superintendents.*

JOHN BUTTERFIELD,
President.

The Overland Mail route went from St. Louis to Fort Smith, Arkansas, and from there through Texas, New Mexico, and Arizona. Stages traveled roughly 2,800 miles and stopped at 139 way stations.

Pulled by four to six stout horses, Concord stages like this heavily laden vehicle crisscrossed the West providing public transportation before rail service became available. In the more remote regions of the West, stages continued to carry passengers until the rise of the automobile in the early twentieth century.

Known as the Stagecoach King, Ben Holladay (1819–1887) took over the mail-carrying operation from William Russell and his partners. At its peak, the Holladay Overland Mail and Express Company operated 20,000 vehicles and employed 14,000 people in providing stagecoach service across 5,000 miles.

Although Butterfield's stage line finally provided the young nation with regular ground mail to the West Coast (as opposed to sending mail by ship), users wanted even faster mail service. That demand was the genesis in 1860 of the Pony Express, operated by William H. Russell, Alexander Majors, and William Waddell. The old Pony Express barn still stood in St. Joseph, Missouri, as late as 1937, when this photograph was taken.

Since a man on a horse could cover ground much faster than a heavy wagon, the Pony Express used a relay system for riders, who carried the mail in sturdy leather saddle bags called mochillas. The company sought young, slim men willing to risk their scalp for $125 a month while agreeing to swear not to drink, curse, or fight with other riders. One of the riders was Frank E. Weber, shown here in 1861.

Edward Creighton (1820–1874), while working for the Pacific Telegraph Company, supervised the building of the first telegraph line from Omaha, Nebraska, to the West Coast starting in the summer of 1860. On October 24, 1861, the first transcontinental telegraph crackled over the wire from California to Washington.

George Francis Train (1829–1904) could not have been more aptly named. A wealthy businessman from Boston, Train helped organize and promote the Union Pacific Railroad in the 1860s. He played an important part in acquiring right-of-way for the first transcontinental railroad and otherwise promoted its construction. An increasingly eccentric character as he aged, a year after the railroad was completed in 1869 Train traveled around the world, his second circumnavigation of the globe. The journey would inspire Jules Verne's classic novel *Around the World in Eighty Days.* Ten years later, Train would do it again—this time in 67 days.

Construction of the Union Pacific transcontinental line began on July 10, 1865, only a few months after the end of the Civil War. By the fall of 1866, when this image was recorded, the tracks extended some 247 miles west from Omaha, Nebraska. The six men standing under the sign are directors of the railroad.

Thomas C. Durant (1820–1885) was vice-president and general manager of the Union Pacific Company and president of Credit Mobilier, the company created to provide supplies for the unprecedented construction project. Durant, the company, and many of its stockholders were crooked, and the two words "Credit Mobilier" eventually became synonymous with the nineteenth century's greatest financial scandal. But the nation got rail service from coast to coast.

Grenville M. Dodge (1831–1916), originally from Massachusetts, earned a degree in civil engineering in Vermont and then settled in Iowa in 1851. He served as a Union officer in the Civil War, but left the Army to oversee construction of the Union Pacific Railroad. As the Union Pacific's tracks moved west, workers laid rails eastward from California for an eventual connection that would tie the nation together by rail.

The east-bound and west-bound tracks connected at Promontory, Utah, amid grand festivities on May 10, 1869. Other giddy celebrations occurred elsewhere across the country as word spread by telegraph that the nation finally had a transcontinental rail line. Soon, it would be possible to travel from New York to San Francisco in just eight days, the transportation miracle of the era.

Wearing a fashionable 1880s-vintage hat, a well-dressed young woman poses for the camera as she sits on a side saddle. In the Old West, it was considered immodest for a woman to ride astride a horse. This photograph was taken in New Mexico in the mid-1880s.

With the discovery of gold in the Black Hills of South Dakota, a lot of people suddenly had urgent business in Deadwood. That naturally proved to be a boon for the stagecoach business. One of the most famous routes connected Cheyenne, Wyoming, and Deadwood, South Dakota, a distance of 300 miles. Hostile Indians and gangs of robbers were a continuing problem for the stage operators.

"Deadwood Dick" was a popular character in the dime novels published during the last quarter of the nineteenth century and a lot of real people adopted that handle as their nickname. One of them was Richard W. Clark, a noted stagecoach driver during Deadwood, South Dakota's heyday as a gold rush town in the mid-1870s.

While stagecoaches and railroads handled most long-distance travel in the West, the horse and buggy remained a mainstay of
local transportation until the advent of the so-called horseless carriage—the automobile. This rig was photographed in the 1880s
in Hillsboro, New Mexico Territory.

THE CIVILIZERS

Settling a land does not immediately bring with it civilization. As America spread toward the Pacific, it required the U.S. military along with militia-like groups such as the Texas Rangers and determined volunteers to make the West relatively safe from hostile Indians and raiders from Mexico. While the morality of that continues to be debated by historians, it was a process that lasted until 1891 when the infamous blood-letting at Wounded Knee marked the end of the American Indian wars.

While the military coped with the Indians, civilian authorities developed and maintained a criminal justice system in the new western states and territories. Local, state, and federal lawmen delivered many an outlaw into the court system or killed those who forcibly resisted arrest. Prosecutors presented cases, juries weighed evidence, and judges interpreted the law and passed sentences.

But civilization is more than public safety supported by the rule of law. Doctors trained back East, or in Europe, extended medical care (not that the Old West didn't have its share of quacks and snake oil salesmen); teachers and professors brought instruction; ministers, priests, and rabbis brought religion; and journalists and writers provided the flow of information necessary for a democracy.

Some would say the West would never have been civilized had it not been for the women. The West had its bad women as well as bad men, but as wives, mothers, or sisters, women in the West raised children, pushed for better schools, started libraries, organized cultural events, and campaigned for temperance while some of them demanded and finally won for women the right to vote, own property, and serve on juries.

Major General William Tecumseh Sherman (1820–1891), seated third from left facing the camera, is better known for his Civil War exploits, but as the Army's ranking officer following the rebellion, he oversaw the military's efforts to deal with Indians across the West. This image was taken when he met with an assemblage of Northern Plains Indian chiefs at Fort Laramie, Wyoming Territory, in 1868.

The Modoc War, the westernmost of the Indian conflicts that marked the settlement of the West, took place in southern Oregon and northern California in 1872-73. Seated at right is Alex McKay, a correspondent for the *San Francisco Bulletin*. Two armed scouts crouch behind a piled-rock buttress at left.

Having no trouble being able to assume an in-charge posture, Lieutenant Colonel George Armstrong Custer poses for a photographer. For obvious reasons, his men called him "Old Curly" behind his back. This image was recorded by Mathew Brady in 1865.

The year his Army colleagues concluded the bloody Modoc campaign in the Pacific Northwest, Custer is shown sitting in his trophy-filled office at Fort Abraham Lincoln at what is now Bismarck, North Dakota.

Following Spread: Two days before the Fourth of July in 1874, Lieutenant Colonel Custer rode out of Fort Abraham Lincoln for the Black Hills of South Dakota. What came to be known as the Black Hills Expedition included 12 companies of soldiers, 61 Indian scouts, 16 musicians, 4 scientists, 3 journalists, 1 photographer, and 2 miners. In addition, the expedition had a field gun and three Gatling guns. Custer and his scouts led the way while a battalion of infantry guarded the rear. The 1874 expedition included 110 canvas-topped supply wagons.

The size of Custer's command is evident in this view of his camp at Hidden Wood Creek. His orders were to scout for a good location for a new military installation in the Black Hills, but two miners were along to investigate rumors of great mineral wealth in the area that included the sprawling Sioux Reservation.

Never one to draw too keen a distinction between business and pleasure, Custer (center) killed this grizzly bear in the Black Hills. When he returned to Fort Abraham Lincoln on July 22, 1874, he carried news that the miners on the expedition had indeed found traces of gold.

A camping and hunting party of soldiers, their wives, and friends on the Little Heart River near Fort Lincoln in 1875. Custer, wearing his trademark buckskin, stands in the center with his arms crossed.

In the best-known military engagement in Old West history, Custer led the Seventh Cavalry into disaster near the Little Big Horn River in Montana on June 25, 1876. Custer's strategy of attacking a large Sioux village backfired and he found himself facing several thousand warriors with only 215 soldiers. The cocky young officer and all of his command died that day. In that and other engagements, 51 percent of the entire Seventh Cavalry were killed. This is one of many fanciful artistic conceptions of the bloody debacle.

A year after the massacre of Custer and his men, all that remained on the lonely battlefield were heaps of horse bones.

The original grave markers for the slaughtered men of Custer's command. The wooden cross at center marks the "Boy General's" final resting place.

President Ulysses S. Grant called Ranald S. MacKenzie (1840–1889) the Army's "most promising young officer" and as an Indian fighter, MacKenzie did not disappoint. He played an important role in the 1874-75 Red River War, a campaign that broke the will of the Comanche and Kiowas in Texas. MacKenzie became mentally ill in 1883 and was retired from the Army a year later.

Two cut trees form a makeshift stretcher, pulled by two horses to remove a wounded man from the scene of the Battle of Slim Buttes in the Dakota Territory. U.S. Cavalry troopers tangled with Sioux warriors September 9-10, 1876—the Army's first significant victory since the Custer massacre earlier that summer.

Illinois-born James Butler Hickok (1837–1876) grew up on the Kansas frontier. A fancy dresser and good shot fond of gambling, Hickok earned his Will Bill nickname in an 1861 shooting fray that left three people dead. He rode as an Army scout and served as a deputy U.S. marshal before gaining the job that won him lasting fame as city marshal of rough and tough Abilene, Kansas.

Wild Bill Hickok spent eight busy months as marshal of Abilene, Kansas, in 1871 in its last season as a cattle town. He was friends with Buffalo Bill Cody (at right) and Texas Jack Omohundro (standing) and performed with Cody early in his career as a showman. Wild Bill's luck as a gambler finally ran out August 2, 1876, when someone shot him to death as he sat playing poker in Deadwood, South Dakota.

In one of the more unusual photographs from the Old West, C. H. "Colorado Charley" Utter and his brother Steve (at left) are visiting the fresh grave of Wild Bill Hickok. Charley, an old friend of Wild Bill's, put up the white wooden marker in memory of Bill.

First envisioned by Texas colonizer Stephen F. Austin, who proposed hiring 10 men "for the common defense" of his fledgling colony, by 1874 the Texas Rangers had evolved into a mounted state constabulary. They had fought Indians for more than half a century, but in the mid-1870s they converted to criminal law enforcement.

Bat Masterson (1853–1921) looked like a dandy as a young man, but he served his western apprenticeship as a buffalo hunter—not a delicate occupation. In 1877, he got elected as sheriff of Ford County, Kansas. The county seat was one of the most famous towns of the Old West, Dodge City. His earned reputation as a gunman made it easy for him to land jobs in law enforcement, though he also gambled, ran saloons, and promoted boxing.

At 49, Bat Masterson left the west for New York. He gained appointment as a deputy U.S. marshal from President Theodore Roosevelt, but lost the job when President William Howard Taft took office. At the urging of a friend, Masterson wrote a series of magazine articles about the Wild West characters he had known, and got a job as a sportswriter for the *New York Morning Telegraph*. He died of a heart attack sitting at his newsroom desk in October 1921.

Tom Horn (1860–1903) worked as cowboy and miner, helped the U.S. Army trail hostile Apaches, and served as a deputy sheriff in the Arizona Territory. But while working as a range detective for the Wyoming Cattleman's Association, he was accused of killing a 14-year-old boy, the son of a sheepman. Though some believe he was framed, that didn't prevent his being hanged for murder.

While Tom Horn went from good guy to bad guy, Frank Canton (1849–1927) did the opposite. Born in Virginia, he grew up in Texas as Joseph Horner. He killed a man in a barroom fight and became an outlaw. Fleeing the Lone Star state in the late 1870s, he went to Wyoming and changed his name to Frank M. Canton. The former outlaw got elected sheriff of Johnson County and spent most of the rest of his life as a lawman in Wyoming, Oklahoma, Alaska, and Texas, where he eventually gained a pardon.

Isaac Charles Parker (1836–1896), better known as "the Hanging Judge," was appointed to the federal bench at Fort Smith, Arkansas, by President U. S. Grant on May 10, 1875. Parker's district included the adjacent Indian Territory, a haven for outlaws. The judge sentenced 161 men to death (88 of them hanged, the others prevailing on appeal or otherwise avoiding execution) during a 21-year career that ended with his death on November 17, 1896.

Ten deputy U.S. marshals who worked in Judge Parker's district in the 1880s and 1890s. Back row, from the left, are Wes Bauman, Abe Allen, John Tolbit, Bill Smith, and Tom Johnson. Front row, from left, Dave Rusk, Heck Bruner, Paden Colbert, Charles Copeland, and G. S. White.

George Maledon looked as dour as his profession would suggest. In addition to his duties as a deputy U.S. marshal, he wound up as hangman for Judge Parker's court at Fort Smith, executing around 60 men. Maledon would retire to an old soldiers home in Johnson City, Tennessee, where he died of natural causes in 1911.

A stout rope had a civilizing influence all across the West. In this image, a soldier of the Eighth Infantry tried for murder by civilian authorities at Prescott, Arizona Territory, in 1877 listens to a final prayer before the trap is sprung.

Isaac Parker aside, "Judge Lynch" ranked as the most famous jurist in the West. From gold-booming San Francisco to the piney woods of East Texas, citizens frequently took the law into their own hands. In this image, one John Heith dangles from a telegraph pole on February 22, 1884, for his suspected role in a robbery in Tombstone, Arizona Territory, that left four people dead. Five others were legally hanged for the crime.

Though legal, the hanging of outlaw Thomas Edward "Black Jack" Ketchum (1863–1901) at Clayton, New Mexico Territory, on April 26, 1901, was messy. Moments after this photograph was taken, Ketchum dropped through the trap. Unfortunately, whoever calculated the drop figured incorrectly. Instead of breaking the condemned man's neck, the rope decapitated him.

In the vastness of the West, criminals often found incarceration quite confining. This small yet sturdily constructed jail was in use in the Wyoming Territory when this image was recorded in 1893.

The jail in Clifton, Arizona Territory, consisted of a series of cells blasted out of solid rock in 1881 by the owners of the nearby copper mines. The blasting was done by one Margarito Barela, who when he got drunk and "shot up" the town, had the honor of being the lockup's first prisoner.

Patrick Floyd Garrett (1850–1908) was born in Alabama but grew up in Louisiana. In 1869, he came to Texas to work as a cowboy in Dallas County. Garrett took up buffalo hunting for a time in West Texas, but returned to cowpunching in the Texas Panhandle in 1877. He then drifted to Lincoln County in New Mexico in 1879 and became sheriff in 1880. A year later he gunned down the young outlaw called Billy the Kid, earning lasting fame if not unanimous respect.

Patrick Garrett, seated at left, posed for this studio portrait with two other but lesser-known onetime sheriffs of Lincoln County: James Brent, standing, and John W. Poe, seated at right. An 1882 ghost-written book on Billy the Kid and his terminal role in the gunman's career made Garrett famous.

Unable to get elected again in New Mexico either as a sheriff or state senator, Pat Garrett left the territory in 1884 and returned to the Texas Panhandle, where he led a company of private rangers to combat cattle rustling. In that capacity, Garrett is shown in this image at right, seated. Others in the photograph are, standing from left, W. S. Mabry, Frank James, C. B. Vivian, and Ike P. Ryland. Seated from left are James H. East and James E. McMasters.

This .44-caliber single-action Colt revolver was carried for a time by Billy the Kid. The outlaw lost the gun on December 21, 1880, when Sheriff Pat Garrett and his posse arrested him at Stinking Springs in New Mexico Territory. The Kid escaped custody in April 1881, but that July, Garrett caught up with him again, this time ensuring that the Kid would never need to worry about getting a new sidearm.

By 1880, former Dodge City lawman Wyatt Earp and his five brothers had gathered in the new mining boom town of Tombstone, Arizona Territory—one of the most appropriately named places in the West. Failing to gain election as sheriff of Cochise County, Wyatt worked the gambling tables at the Oriental Saloon while older brother Virgil served as town marshal.

Virgil W. Earp (1843–1905), the second oldest of the Earp brothers, was the law in Tombstone, but he and brothers Wyatt and Morgan and their supporters became increasingly at odds with small ranchers in the area, particularly N. H. "Old Man" Clanton and his three sons, Ike, Phin, and Billy.

Morgan Earp (1851–1882) had worked as a lawman in Dodge City. He came to Tombstone from Butte, Montana, and got a job as a shotgun messenger for Wells Fargo. Morgan was shot to death in March 1882 as he played a game of pool, his unknown assailants never apprehended.

The bad blood between the Clantons and the Earps, particularly Wyatt, grew more toxic with time. On October 26, 1881, believing the Clantons intended violence, Marshal Virgil Earp deputized brothers Wyatt and Morgan and a family friend, Doc Holliday, to arrest them. When the Earps and Holliday ran into Ike, Tom, and Billy Clanton along with Frank and Tom McLaury, friends of the Clantons, shooting started. In a matter of seconds, the McLaury brothers and Billy Clanton lay dead, with Virgil and Morgan Earp wounded. The fight happened near Tombstone's O.K. Corral, shown here, and the gunfight took on that name.

Dallas Stoudenmire (1845–1882) was an honest lawman, but as one writer later put it, he "drank too much and shot too fast." As city marshal of rough-and-tumble El Paso in 1881, he earned a reputation as a solid town-tamer. The trigger-happy Stoudenmire, shown standing, resigned his city job and got appointed as a deputy U.S. marshal in 1882. That September, two men he had been feuding with since his service as city marshal killed Stoudenmire in a gunfight.

By 1883, the Kansas cow town of Dodge City had quieted down considerably. But when Mayor Alonzo Webster (who owned two saloons) hypocritically moved to run gamblers and competing saloon men out of town, rival saloon owner Luke Short called on his friend lawman-gambler Bat Masterson for support in what came to be called the Dodge City War. The two men formed the so-called Dodge City Peace Commission, a group of not particularly peaceful men. Standing, from left, are William H. Harris, Short, and Masterson. Seated, from the left, are Charles Bassett, Wyatt Earp, M. F. McClain, and Neal Brown. A sympathetic constable deputized them so they could legally pack pistols.

Like many Western lawmen, John Henry Selman (1839–1896) had a shady past. Involved in vigilantism in the Fort Griffin, Texas, vicinity in the 1870s, Selman drifted to New Mexico and got involved in the Lincoln County War. Back in Texas, he landed in El Paso and got a job as a deputy sheriff and later won election as a constable.

What made Selman famous was gunning down John Wesley Hardin, one of the West's most prolific killers, in August 1895. Less than a year later, Selman was shot to death in an El Paso alley.

In considering Old West military figures, George Crook (1828–1890) was unusual in that he proved to be both a worthy foe and sometimes friend to the Indians the nation displaced as it grew toward the Pacific. Born in Ohio, he saw his first Indian campaigns in the Pacific Northwest in the 1850s. Crook then fought with skill in the Civil War.

His trademark mutton chops somewhat grayer after the war between the North and South, George Crook returned to the Pacific Northwest for service. The Indians called him Natan Lupan—Gray Wolf. In 1871, the Army ordered him to Arizona Territory to deal with hostile Apaches.

Not looking particularly martial in a heavy coat and civilian hat, George Crook succeeded in getting the Apaches to a reservation and bringing relative calm to Arizona by 1873. In 1875, he was named commander of the Department of the Platt, which included the Black Hills of South Dakota, spiritual home to the Sioux. In the Battle of Rosebud on June 17, 1876, Crook endured his only combat loss, a strategic victory for the Sioux that probably contributed to Custer's coming bad luck.

Valentine T. McGillycuddy (1849–1939), shown here with General Crook's expedition to the Black Hills in 1876, served as a surgeon and surveyor for the group. He would also serve at Fort Robinson and for the Red Cloud Agency, befriending Crazy Horse. McGillycuddy wound up as the mayor of Rapid City, South Dakota, and South Dakota's first state surgeon general.

This was General Crook's field headquarters at Whitewood during the Dakota campaigns of 1876. Pursuing a party of Indians with elements of the Third and Fifth Cavalry, the general's command ran out of provisions. Before making it back to the relative civilization of Deadwood, the soldiers were forced to eat many of their horses.

General Crook's efforts succeeded in getting the Apaches back to their reservation, but the peace lasted only a couple of years. In 1884, Apaches under a headman named Geronimo once again broke from their reservation and Crook again went on their trail. He is shown here with two scouts, Bakeetz-ogie (Yellow Coyote) and Al-Che-Say, chief of Crook's White Mountain Scouts. Unconventional, Crook used a mule instead of a horse, chose civilian attire better suited than uniforms to coping with the rugged landscape, and carried a double-barreled, 10-gauge shotgun in lieu of the standard-issue rifle.

Some Indians were heroes, at least from the white man's perspective. This is General Crook's chief scout, the Apache Al-Che-Say. Using Indians to fight Indians was one of Crook's innovative tactics. Crook used Indian scouts, fought only when he had to, and tried to treat with the Indians rather than exterminate them. He viewed the nation's ongoing Indian woes as the consequence of "tardy and broken faith on the part of the general government." In 1882, the general was sent back to Arizona, where the Apaches had fled their reservation at San Carlos and resumed their depredations.

The U.S. Army created four African-American regiments in 1866—the Twenty-fourth and Twenty-fifth Infantry and the Ninth and Tenth Cavalry. The black soldiers were commanded by white officers. The Indians, who quickly learned they were hard fighters, called them Buffalo Soldiers. This is a group of soldiers from the Twenty-fifth Infantry, taken at Fort Keogh, Montana, in 1890.

Though the popular image is that the U.S. Cavalry stood ever-ready to charge at the first sound of the bugle, it took training—for men and their horses—to be ready to fight. In this image, a trooper practices laying down his horse and using it for cover as he fires his black-powder Springfield rifle over the animal's ears while officers look on. This photograph was taken around 1885 while the Sixth Cavalry was stationed at Fort Bayard, New Mexico Territory.

Company B, Tenth Infantry, crosses the Gila River around 1885 near the San Carlos Indian Reservation in Arizona Territory.

Crook campaigned hard against the Apaches in 1886, rounding up all but Geronimo and 41 of his followers. Here the general is shown meeting with the wily chief in Mexico on March 17, 1886, in an effort to get him to give up. When Geronimo chose not to return to the reservation, the Army ordered Crook replaced by General Nelson A. Miles. Not long after Miles took command, Geronimo decided to surrender and was shipped off to Florida.

General Nelson A. Miles (1839–1925) grew up in his native Massachusetts, where his parents farmed. But the young man's strong ambitions were not geared toward agriculture. Self-taught in the military arts, he served as a volunteer officer in the Civil War. At war's end, he assumed a colonelcy in the regular Army and relentlessly moved up in rank, ever jealous of the West Pointers he competed against.

Miles was not enthusiastic about transferring from the Pacific Northwest, where he commanded the Department of Columbia, to Arizona. But his strategy of guarding water holes and mountain passes, aided by near-instant communication provided by a network of heliograph stations, finally forced Geronimo to surrender. Though General Crook had done much of the groundwork, Miles happily took the credit.

General Nelson A. Miles later in his distinguished military career. Between 1876 and 1877, Miles assisted the campaign in the Little Big Horn region following Custer's defeat.

Apache prisoners being taken east from Arizona Territory to Florida sit for a photographer at a rest stop near the Nueces River in South Texas on September 10, 1886. They were transported by railroad on the Southern Pacific Line. Geronimo sits in the front row, third from right.

The Battle of Wounded Knee, more accurately a massacre, took place on December 29, 1890, at Wounded Knee Creek on the Pine Ridge Reservation in South Dakota. The incident was the result of an attempt by Seventh Cavalry soldiers to disarm a group of Indians and ended with 146 Indian dead and 51 wounded. The army lost 25 soldiers killed and 39 wounded. The tragic event marked the last of the great bloodletting of the Indian Wars. Here scouts who participated in the fight are returning to their encampment through the snow.

Two cavalry officers survey a vast Sioux Indian camp near the Pine Ridge Reservation in 1891.

Three former Indian warriors relegated to reservation life pose for a photographer.

With Buffalo Bill Cody at center and his press agent John M. Burke at far-right, a mixed group of Pine Ridge Agency Indians and U.S. officials pose for photographer John C. H. Grabill on January 16, 1891. Less than a month after the Wounded Knee trouble, the last of the militant Indians had surrendered. The man at lower left, likely a correspondent for the newspaper, is pointing to the New York World pennant held by two clearly dispirited Indians.

William Matthew Tilghman, Jr. (1854–1924) grew up in Kansas, where at 20 he became a buffalo hunter. Despite a few brushes with the law, by 30 he had taken up law enforcement as a career. In 1889, he settled in Oklahoma, serving variously as a deputy U.S. marshal, municipal police chief, county sheriff, and city marshal. This image, with Deputy U.S. Marshal Charles F. Colcord on the right, was recorded in 1893.

An older Tilghman as Oklahoma City's chief of police in 1912. In 1924, while marshal of Cromwell, Oklahoma, Tilghman would be shot to death in the line of duty.

Chris Madsen (1851–1944), born in Denmark, came to the U.S. in 1876 and immediately enlisted in the Army, where he served with the Fifth Cavalry for 15 years. He suffered wounds in the 1890 Indian fight at Wounded Knee and got left for dead. Madsen recovered and later became a deputy U.S. marshal working out of Fort Smith, Arkansas. With Bill Tilghman and Heck Thomas, Madsen would achieve legendary status as one of the Three Guardsmen.

Heck Thomas (1850–1912), Georgia born, came to Texas with his family in 1875 and worked as a railroad guard and later as a detective before joining the U.S. Marshal's Service in 1886. He worked in Indian Territory along with Tilghman and Madsen. Thomas soon had a reputation as a standout lawman, but he gained even more acclaim for ending the career of the outlaw Bill Doolin, a bank robber whose criminal record traced back to membership in the Dalton gang. Thomas found Doolin on his farm near Lawton, Oklahoma, on August 26, 1896, and killed him in a gunfight.

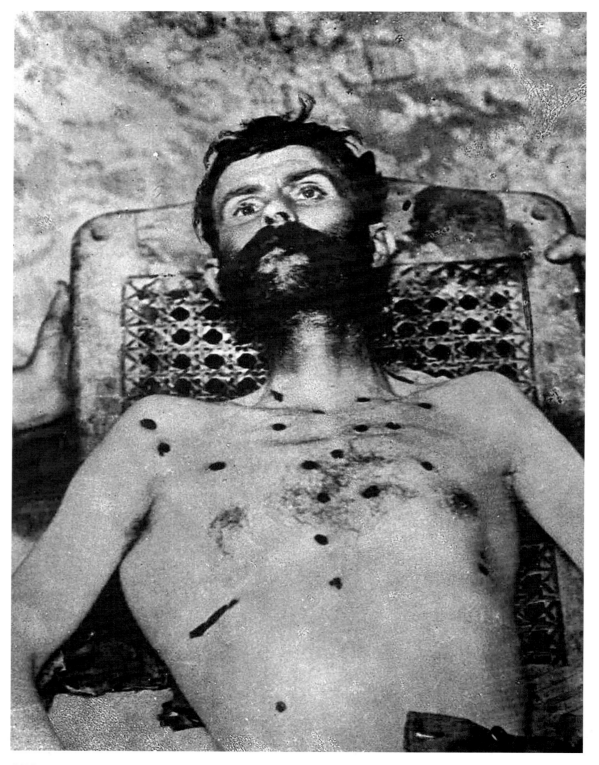

Bill Doolin was no western hero, but the man who shot him—Heck Thomas—certainly was. Thomas was said to have killed 11 outlaws during his long service as a federal lawman.

Jeff D. Milton (1861–1947) had a life that would have made a good Hollywood Western. Born in Florida, he came to Texas when he was 15 to work as a cowboy and later cut his law enforcement teeth as a Texas Ranger. He went on to spend a long career as a local, county, state, and federal officer in Texas, New Mexico, and Arizona. In 1932, he retired in Tombstone, Arizona, where he spent the rest of his life. Shown at right is Frank M. King, an old-time cowboy who spent the last years of his life writing about the Old West.

John Sontag and partner Chris Evans specialized in robbing trains in California and occasionally back in their home territory of Minnesota. They proved extremely hard to catch, in one encounter killing two officers (including a former Texas Ranger) before escaping. But their luck ran out on June 11, 1893, when a posse of local and federal officers found them near Stone Corral, California. Sontag was mortally wounded in the shootout that followed. Evans was also badly wounded and captured a short time later. Sontag died the following July 3 of tetanus, but Evans survived to serve time in prison.

Wilson N. Jones (1827?–1901), in the foreground with watch fob and wearing a high-crowned hat, served as governor of the Choctaw Nation in Indian Territory (Oklahoma) from 1890 to 1894. At one point he had to use a force known as the Choctaw Light Horsemen to put down a virtual civil war. During his administration, Jones also pushed for better education for his people.

Charles Fred Lambert (1887–1971) was born during a blizzard in the hotel his parents ran in Cimarron, New Mexico Territory. Buffalo Bill Cody, who happened to be staying there that night, suggested that the baby be named "Cyclone" and the nickname stuck. At 16, Lambert became the youngest-ever person to serve as a territorial marshal, the beginning of a 36-year career of government service.

Soldiers and lawmen did much to tame the West, but women facilitated full civilization in raising families, providing education, and bringing cultural amenities like libraries, musical societies, and study clubs. This woman, her name lost to time, poses in her best dress and finest hat for a professional photographer in New Mexico Territory in the mid-1880s.

Alice Cunningham Fletcher (1838–1923) was a noted ethnologist who specialized in American Indian civilizations. Beyond her scholarly work, in 1883 she served as a special agent in allotting land to the Omaha tribes and four years later again worked as a federal special agent in distributing land to the Nez Perce and Winnebago tribes. In this image, she stands at left looking over documents with Nez Perce men and government surveyors.

Dr. Susan Anderson (1870–1960) was born in Fort Wayne, Indiana, but moved to Cripple Creek, Colorado, with her family when she was a young woman. She left there in 1893 to study medicine at the University of Michigan, where she graduated in 1897. Returning to Colorado, she spent most of the rest of her life caring for miners, railroad workers, loggers, and others in her adopted state. Here she is shown standing outside her log cabin at Cripple Creek shortly before she left for Michigan. The two men are not identified.

A company of Texas Rangers pose with their Winchesters in South Texas in the mid-1880s.

Texas Ranger Bazz Outlaw (whose conduct resembled that name) made a fine lawman—provided he was sober. His career ended violently in El Paso on April 6, 1894, when he got drunk, killed another Ranger, and was himself gunned down by Constable John Selman.

Deputy U.S. Marshal Heck Thomas later in his career. The Three Guardsmen—Bill Tilghman, Chris Madsen, and Heck Thomas—were credited with the apprehension of hundreds of bad men during the 1890s. Thomas would end his career as first chief of police of Lawton, Oklahoma, dying in 1912 of Bright's disease.

Three old-time Oklahoma characters pose for a photographer in Houston in 1937. At left is E. D. Nix, U.S. Marshal for Oklahoma; at center is Al Jennings, a onetime bank and train robber who portrayed himself as a much more notorious outlaw than he really was; and former Deputy U.S. Marshal Chris Madsen.

Eastern-born, Theodore Roosevelt (1858–1919) came West in 1884 to ranch in the Dakota Territory following the death of his mother and first wife. He stayed only a couple of years, but his trek marked the beginning of the future president's lifelong interest in the West. In 1898, he organized the famed volunteer cavalry unit known as the Rough Riders, in San Antonio. Here the outfit is camped at the old fairgrounds.

Some of the appeal of the Old West to myth-makers was that much of it needed no embellishment. From the mile-deep Grand Canyon in Arizona to the 300-foot-tall giant sequoias of California to the geysers and bubbling mud pots of Yellowstone, truth was truly stranger than fiction. Here in 1886, a group of officers and guests take lunch beneath a giant cactus near Fort Thomas in Arizona Territory.

PURVEYORS OF THE MYTH

America's Western myth began taking shape well before the Old West had been tamed. In the summer of 1869, a writer named Edward Zane Carroll Judson left the comforts of the Eastern seaboard for North Platte, Nebraska, looking for new story material. Judson was hardly a household name, but almost anyone who could read recognized his pseudonym, Ned Buntline. As a prolific dime novelist, Buntline became America's top-earning author.

The Indian fighter whom Judson hoped to interview—Wild Bill Hickok—declined to talk, but he suggested someone who might: A young scout named William F. Cody. Judson had no trouble inducing Cody to loosen his tongue and collected ample material for his next piece of fiction, *Buffalo Bill, the King of Border Men.* In 1870, Bret Harte published *The Luck of Roaring Camp and Other Sketches.* The book, a roundup of stories from his days as a reporter in booming San Francisco, is a funny yet sympathetic portrayal of frontier types. He created a range of Western stereotypes that endure to this day. Two years later, Mark Twain (Samuel Clemens), who also had worked as a journalist in San Francisco, came out with *Roughing It.* The book, a funny but slightly fictionalized memoir of the author's days in the West, further added to the Western myth. But it was Twain's earlier story, first published in 1865, that launched his rise to fame. *The Notorious Jumping Frog of Calaveras County* recounted the adventures of Jim Smiley, a miner addicted to gambling in a California gold camp, who pits his uncommonly talented frog in a jumping contest against a frog he fetches for a stranger.

In 1872, Buffalo Bill Cody played himself in Buntline's stage hit, "The Scouts of the Plains." Having tried show business and liked it, in 1874 Cody put together his first Wild West Show at the Omaha fairgrounds. He used real cowboys and Indians to act out a cattle roundup, a stagecoach robbery, and various other events that while still fairly routine in much of the West, would soon prove fascinating to audiences back East and in Europe.

While the Western myth already stood secure, writer Owen Wister codified it in 1902 with his classic novel, *The Virginian.* Though Wister came from the East, his book firmly entrenched the myth of the romantic cowboy life and established the ultimate Western hero, the strong, silent Westerner who famously said, "When you call me that, smile!"—gilded for the big screen by Hollywood as "Smile when you say that!"

Journalists transformed many a Western figure into a hero, sometimes at the cost of their own life. Twenty-two-year-old Harvard graduate Frederick Wadsworth Loring came west to chronicle the Wheeler expedition in 1871, but on his return East to write of all his many adventures Apaches attacked his stagecoach near Wickenburg, Arizona Territory, and killed him along with five others. The young journalist, shown here only 48 hours before his death, leans on his mule Evil Merodach to have his photograph taken.

Surrounded by wagon parts and canyon vistas, a man in the West could experience divided sympathies: How to contemplate the grandeur of his magnificent surroundings versus how to reassemble his wheels. The Canyon de Chelly seems to be inspiring the imagination of this fellow with ample material for yarns.

William Frederick Cody was born in 1846 and lived with his family in this two-story farm house in LeClaire, Iowa. In 1867-68, as a young man with a contract to supply buffalo meat for workers on the Union Pacific Railroad, he earned the nickname that would stay with him the rest of his life: Buffalo Bill. The LeClaire house was later moved to Cody, Wyoming, the town Cody founded.

A youthful Buffalo Bill in his heyday as a scout. At 15, he had gone to work as a rider for the Pony Express. Once, having finished his 116-mile route between Red Buttes Station on the North Platte River and the next station at Tree Crossings, he learned that his relief rider was dead. Cody saddled another of the 21 horses he would use on that ride and covered another 76 miles to the Rocky Ridge Station. Then he turned around and rode back to Red Buttes, a trip of 384 miles in less than 22 hours.

After meeting with Cody, writer Ned Buntline made the soon-to-be-famous scout the hero of one of his dime novels. In 1872, Buntline persuaded Cody to play himself in a stage production, "Scouts of the Plains," based on the book. From the left are Buntline, Cody, and another frontier character, J. B. "Texas Jack" Omohundro.

Believed to have been photographed in 1874, only the identity of the three men in the middle of this image is incontrovertible: Wild Bill Hickok (second from left), Buffalo Bill Cody (at center, hat festooned with ostrich plumes), and Texas Jack Omohundro (fourth from left). The man at far-left is believed to be Eugene Overton and the man on the far right is thought to be Elisha Green.

Behind every great performer are the money men and promoters. Hamming it up during a performance of Buffalo Bill's Wild West Show at Earl's Court in England in the summer of 1892 are, from left, Nate Salsbury, owner and manager of the show, artist-writer Frederick Remington, and John Burke, the show's press agent.

Buffalo Bill may well have the distinction of being the most photographed figure in the history of the Old West. Shown at left standing next to Cody is Gordon William Lillie, better known as "Pawnee Bill." Lillie had been an interpreter for the Pawnee scouts in Cody's Wild West Show, but in 1888 went out on his own with a show he called Pawnee Bill's Historic Wild West. Eventually the two teamed up for a time.

While Buffalo Bill Cody reigned as the personification of the western hero, Phoebe Ann Moses (1860–1926) became the living symbol of the western woman. Far better known by her stage name of Annie Oakley, she learned to shoot as a young girl and by the time she was a teenager she was good enough to perform in exhibitions. Oakley joined Buffalo Bill's troupe in 1885 for 16 seasons. Sitting Bull called her Watanya Cicilia— Little Sure Shot.

Most of the images taken of Annie Oakley showed her in her show costume, often with a firearm. In this photograph from 1889, Oakley is shown loading a gun.

In summer 1892, a blanket-clad Indian watches as Annie Oakley makes a left-handed shot at a target thrown up into the air during a performance of Buffalo Bill's Wild West Show at Earl's Court in England.

Billy Johnson was another of Buffalo Bill Cody's Wild West Show performers. As the show's script put it, "Mr. Billy Johnson will illustrate the mode of riding the Pony Express, mounting, dismounting, and changing the mail to fresh horses."

James W. Willoughby (1857–1916), popularly known as Jim Kid, drove a hack for the Deadwood stage line in 1877, cowboyed in Wyoming, and signed on with the Buffalo Bill Wild West Show in 1885. Two years later, he married Lillian Smith at Staten Island, New York. He later performed in the 101 Ranch Wild West Show and appeared in silent Western films.

While Lillian Smith boasted that she could out-shoot Annie Oakley, Oakley replied that Smith managed to shoot well enough for someone with such an ample figure. Smith later performed in the 101 Wild West Show, coloring her skin so she could pose as "Princess Wenona," a Sioux Indian. Unlike Oakley, she died in near obscurity.

Martha Jane Canary (1852–1903) was far better known simply as Calamity Jane. Sensational accounts of her life had her serving as a scout for Custer and involved in other wild exploits. In truth, she seems to have been a hard-drinking sometimes prostitute who embellished her story to aid her later show business career. In doing so, she managed to become one of the most noted females in the Old West.

This is possibly the final photograph of Calamity Jane. Shown in 1903, she is standing at the grave of Wild Bill Hickok, to whom she supposedly had been secretly married. However, no evidence of that has ever been found.

For some years a riverboat pilot on the Mississippi River, after the Civil War disrupted commerce on America's grand waterway, Samuel Clemens and brother Orion headed west on the overland stage. Clemens would wind up as a reporter in San Francisco, and his experiences in the West would provide material to launch his literary career as Mark Twain. When "The Notorious Jumping Frog of Calaveras County" created a sensation back East, Twain was on his way.

Separating myth from reality in telling the story of Judge Roy Bean (1825?–1903) is difficult. Never shying from a fight, he traveled from his native Kentucky to New Orleans, Mexico, California (where a lover cut the rope just in time to save him from hanging), and New Mexico before settling in Texas after the Civil War. Following the railroad into West Texas, he sold booze to railroad workers and travelers and got elected as a justice of the peace in Val Verde County. Legend says Bean hanged horse thieves, but as a justice of the peace he could legally preside only over misdemeanor cases.

In 1902, a year before his death, Bean sits on a horse outside his famed Jersey Lilly Saloon, named in honor of stage actress Lillie Langtry—a woman he doted on from afar but never met. Although Bean would kick the bucket with his infatuation unrequited, the famous actress heard tale of the man and came west to pay her respects.

John R. Abernathy (1876–1941), also known as Catch 'Em Alive Jack, grew up in Sweetwater, Texas. He got his nickname catching wolves alive, a skill that earned him good money from ranchers eager to get rid of the lupine predators. He guided a wolf hunt for President Roosevelt, who appointed him as a deputy U.S. marshal in Oklahoma Territory. Roosevelt helped sustain the Western myth in numerous articles and books.

President Theodore Roosevelt came to San Antonio in 1905 for a reunion of the Rough Riders. After he left the Alamo city, he went to Northwest Texas and Oklahoma Territory to participate in a wolf hunt. The party killed 17 of the animals.

President Theodore Roosevelt loved the Old West, where he spent some formative time in the early 1880s as a young man. After he moved into the White House, he played a giant role in building America's National Park system. Roosevelt is shown here jumping a split-rail fence in 1909.

Looking back on the many characters of the Old West, it almost seems as if a nickname was as fundamental as hat, boots, and shooting iron. Gathered in 1929 for a reunion in Deadwood, South Dakota, are from left, Deadwood Dick, Buckskin Bill, and Idaho Bill. Seated is Buckskin Johnny.

The original caption at the bottom of this image reads, "Bill Drennan [sic], in his frontier toggery, Kit Carson's favorite scout." In truth, William F. Drannan (1832–1913) was an old-timer who saw the Old West but considerably embellished if not downright fictionalized his life in his 1899 book, *Thirty-one Years on the Plains and in the Mountains; or, the Last Voice from the Plains.* Most historians believe his wife actually wrote the book to bring them income in their old age.

St. Louis native Charles Marion Russell (1864–1926) drew and modeled wax as a child, but starting at 16 went to work as a cowboy in Montana. He continued with his art even while living on ranches, slowly turning from full-time cowboy to full-time artist. By 1920, he had arrived and today is one of the most-collected Western artists.

Owen Wister (1860–1938) grew up in Pennsylvania and attended Harvard, but as a fiction writer, he codified the Western myth in his classic novel *The Virginian*. The book contains the most-recognized line in western fiction: "When you call me that, smile!" The line is usually rewritten as, "Smile when you say that!"

Notes on the Photographs

These notes, listed by page number, attempt to include all aspects known of the photographs. Each of the photographs is identified by the page number, photograph's title or description, photographer and collection, archive, and call or box number when applicable. Although every attempt was made to collect all data, in some cases complete data may have been unavailable due to the age and condition of some of the photographs and records.